WHAT IS BITCOIN

unraveling the mystery

Anthony Crafts

Anthony Crafts

CONTENTS

Title Page
Preface
What is money? 1
The Internet 5
Cryptography 9
The Gamers Already Get It 15
The Community 21
What is real? 24
Governments and Banks 26
Planes, Trains, Microchips and Automobiles 30
The Alien Connection 32
Cyber Moolah 36
Books By This Author 39

PREFACE

This is a non-technical description of Bitcoin. In this book I simplify the various aspects of Bitcoin and describe them in an easy to understand format. When you are done reading, will you be able to start your own block chain and create a crypto coin with your name on it? No. For that you would need many books, far more technical than this one. Will you know how to invest in Bitcoin and make millions? Goodness no. If all goes well, you will finish this book and say "Okay, now I get it. So thaaaat's what Bitcoin is."

Before we get into the meat of it, I want to clear up a couple of things. When I say Bitcoin, I am talking about the concept of Bitcoin as a cyber currency. There are many crypto coins with distinct differences and various uses. I am sure many more coins will be created after the publication of this book. Once you have a basic understanding of Bitcoin, you can apply what you learned here to any other coin, even the ones that haven't been created yet.

When I use the term Internet I am talking about the World Wide Web, The Net, the Inter webs, and whatever other term you may use to describe how every computer and smartphone in the world is connected.

If you are reading this book it means you have taken interest in one of the most fascinating concepts in the history of this world. A perfect currency! It comes on the back of other great discoveries including the Internet, torrenting, and advanced cryptography. As you learn more about this subject I promise you will become more and more enthralled with it. This is one subject that becomes more and more interesting as it's investigated. Sometimes, when I pick up a book and start leafing through it I wonder, 'What's the author's real motivation for writing this?'

Here are my primary motivations: Back in 2012 while working as a computer programmer for an awesome company named Visions Beyond I got to work with some amazing people. It was our job to abstract large complex concepts down to easily understood ideas and then build software based on those basic building blocks. I fell in love with the process and that is what I'm doing here in this book. Bitcoin can be confusing, unless we break it down to its fundamentals. Then anyone can understand it.

I deeply wish I had taken the time to learn more

about Bitcoin back in 2012 when I owned dozens of them. Back then they were selling for about $10 a piece. I purchased them, really just so I could tell my friends and family, 'Hey I bought some bitcoins.' They didn't seem impressed, so I sold them. All of them. Then, in 2018 my friend and boss, Matt told me that I could easily buy and sell bitcoin on an investing app called Robinhood. At that time they were selling for about $1,000 each. I thought 'No way am I paying that much for a bitcoin!' With my technical background I should have been the first person on the Bitcoin bandwagon. I just hadn't looked into it enough. Well, now that I've actually done the research and I see the vision of what Bitcoin will become I'm scrambling to buy up just a small fraction of what I once owned and I am convinced that if I had taken the time to sit down and research the topic for just an hour or two it would have been enough to convince me to keep my bitcoins. If this book helps just one person avoid the same mistake I made, it will be worth the effort.

WHAT IS MONEY?

Money is commonly defined as any medium of exchange. Cash isn't the only type of money. Assets, property, and resources can also be considered.

Without a widely accepted medium of exchange, communities resort to something called bartering. There's nothing fundamentally wrong with bartering. It's still practiced, even in a modern society. But when it's the only form of exchange available, it can make life difficult.

Let's say I have a chicken coop and therefore an overabundance of eggs, but I am in need of a new pair of shoes. I am now faced with several difficult tasks. First, I need to find someone who needs eggs. Then I need to find someone who has a pair of shoes to trade, and not just any shoes. They need to be my size and the type of shoe I'm looking for. Once I've found the appropriate people, I need to figure out some way to trade my eggs for the shoes. Maybe the person who needs the eggs doesn't have any shoes to sell, and perhaps the person who has the shoes I want isn't in need of any eggs. Things get complicated. Maybe it takes a few days to make some kind of arrangement between everyone involved. Well, now my eggs are a few days old and they are worth less. Bartering can become very messy, very quickly.

That's why most societies decide very quickly to create some form of money. It just makes life less complicated and allows people to be more productive. I can sell my eggs for money, then use that money to buy my shoes. Simple!

But what do we use for money? And what if some clever fiend decides to create fake money? Well, finding good answers to those questions has perplexed even the most powerful and modern governments.

Many ancient societies used gold as money. It's a beautiful and highly useful metal. It's also rare. It's easy to identify and difficult to counterfeit. Seems like the perfect thing to use, right? Well, it's not. It's very heavy. Carrying a bag of gold around the shopping center just isn't practical. It's difficult to keep safe. If someone is able to accumulate any sizeable amount of gold they become a target for robbery. There's also no way to identify a particular owner of a piece of gold. It's owned by whoever is holding it. Even if that person is a thief. Using gold for money comes with its own set of problems.

I mentioned to my dad that I am writing a book about bitcoin. He thought for a minute and said, 'Well you need to mention salt'.

'Salt?'

'Yes, it's been used as money many times throughout history.'

Sure enough he was right. Salt is actually a fascinating form of currency. It seemed even more perfect than gold in many ways. It's very easy to identify and almost impossible to counterfeit. In ancient times it was an absolute necessity if you wanted to preserve food. So why isn't salt used as money anymore? Well, we are going to talk more about this later in the book, but this simple answer is, it became too abundant. It also became less useful. Once modern refrigeration was invented salt basically became a way to season food, and that's about it. Plus, everyone had plenty of it.

So that's where governments around the world started stepping in. Let's face it, if the people aren't happy, government officials aren't happy. So in an effort to keep things running smoothly governments around the world started creating what is called fiat money.

Simply put, fiat money is currency that is backed by a government rather than a commodity such as gold. Most modern currencies, including the U.S. dollar, are fiat currencies.

I will devote an entire chapter to this subject, but

for now just keep in mind that fiat currency is incredibly flawed. It's expensive to create (especially coins). It's easy to counterfeit. If stolen, it can't be traced back to the proper owner.

THE INTERNET

Now that we've discussed money. Let's talk about the Internet. You might be thinking, 'Hey, Anthony I know what money is and I definitely know about the Internet."
Well, fair enough but I just want to lay some common groundwork. Bitcoin is so amazing that I just want to make sure we start out 'on the same page', sort of speak.

I remember the late 80's when the personal computer was making its way into households everywhere. IBM was at the forefront of this effort. It's amazing to think about now, but IBM actually had a difficult time finding people to work on the PC project. They knew how to make the hardware, but needed to create a robust operating system. IBM sought out several qualified people and asked them to help, promising high wages and even profit sharing options. They got the same reply over and over. 'Nobody will ever want a computer in their house,' the programmers said. 'Computers are for laboratories and offices.' My grandpa used to say 'Sometimes the smartest people make the dumbest decisions.'

But IBM kept searching. Finally, a member of the board of directors said, 'My son could probably write that operating system for you. He's a computer science student.' The IBM director was Mary Gates and her son's name was Bill. You can probably piece together the rest of that story.

So, before everybody knew it, boxes were being opened in living rooms everywhere by excited hands. A spot was chosen in every house for this amazing machine. Desks and chairs were being pulled up from basements and then everyone started asking the same question. 'Other than playing solitaire, what do we use this thing for?'

Well, just in the nick of time, before people started losing interest in this PC they just shelled out a handsome chunk of money for, along came the Internet! Now, the computer in our house could connect to a computer in someone else's house! I remember buying and installing my first high speed modem. I nervously took the cover off the family computer and inserted the device, as the instructions showed. I felt like a mad scientist. Then, I started my first subscription to America Online! Wow! I had arrived! This was amazing! I was chatting with people around the world and downloading information on just about any subject I could think of. Homework was a snap! I didn't have to go to the library anymore. I could look up anything from home! The world was at my fingertips. Then I heard it was possible to start my own webpage and that's when I was truly hooked. I've been in love with the internet and all it's amazing uses ever since.

Here's a true story you probably won't believe, but it's still true. It was October 13, 1994. Halloween was coming. I was downstairs playing on the computer as usual. I had heard that, for a fee, people could have their own domain name. Whatever you could think of, you could make it into an easy to remember internet address. I was checking the names of various well-known companies just to see if they had established their Internet presence yet. They were all taken. Then I typed in 'cocacola.com' and it said 'Available'. I got a cold chill. Did I misspell cocacola? It must be a typo. I checked it over and over. I had it right! I got scared and turned the computer off. The next day I decided to go ahead and buy it. What harm could come? Right? I might be famous! I looked up the domain again and it said 'Taken.' I lost my chance. It's probably for the best though. Coca-Cola probably would have sued me and I was just a kid. I definitely didn't have the money to hire a lawyer, and don't think my parents would have been pleased, or amused.

Well, enough about me. Back to Bitcoin. The reason I tell that story though is to illustrate how something virtual, something that doesn't exist in the real world, like cocacola.com, can have incredible value. I hear people say 'Bitcoin doesn't really exist. There's nothing I can put in my hand.' Well, cocacola.com doesn't really exist. You can't put it in your hand. But if you want to see the real value of a web address to a company lookup www.nissan.com and read that story.

Back in 1994 I was fascinated by the Internet and computers, but in my wildest dreams I never imagined that one day every single person would have a computer a thousand times more powerful than the one I was using, and they would carry it around in their pocket! These pocket held devices would become so important that most people wouldn't be able to take their eyes off of them, not even while driving! That was something I couldn't even imagine at the time, but has now become reality.

I've spent a great deal of time trying to imagine how Bitcoin is going to be used five, ten, even fifty years from now. Will it transform the world like the computer and cell phone have? I personally believe it will have an even greater impact. But more about that later...

CRYPTOGRAPHY

In the third grade my friend Bobby came up with a system that would allow us to pass notes in class without allowing others to read it. He gave me a sheet of paper with the alphabet clearly printed in capital letters. On a second row, directly underneath the same letters were printed again, this time they were scrambled. The sheet of paper he gave me was a 'crypto key'.

A B C D E F G...

R T V N A L M...

Each letter on the first row corresponded to the letter directly underneath it. When I wrote Bobby a note that was to be passed in class I would use the letters on the bottom row. The note made no sense. I had 'encrypted' the note. I could now pass it across the room, person to person, without worry. While the note journeyed across the room from hand to hand anyone who looked at it just smirked and shrugged their shoulders. They couldn't read it. When Bobby received it, he used the same key to 'decrypt' it. It worked perfectly! As we wrote more and more notes we became familiar with the key. It eventually got to the point where we could read and write coded notes without using it.

The term crypto currency simply means a form of money that is kept safe through encryption. Just like a safe or lockbox is used to keep paper money safe, encryption is used to keep Bitcoin safe.

Let's say Bobby and I wanted to create an 'I OWE YOU'. We could write a message that says 'Bobby or Anthony will exchange this paper for ten dollars.' That piece of paper now has real value, but we don't need to hide it or keep it in a safe. We could lay it right on a desk, out in the open. Since Bobby and I are the only ones who can decrypt the message, we are the only ones who can collect on the promise made.

Bitcoin is based on a much more complex cryptography system involving dizzying math equations, private and public keys, torrenting, and many other factors that we won't discuss in this book. The basic principle, however, is the same. Every bitcoin transaction is kept on a public ledger. It's out in the open for anyone to see, and if you want to claim a bitcoin for yourself, all you need is the proper key.

To illustrate the true power of encryption look no

further than the national news. In February, 2016 the FBI asked Apple to assist in cracking the sign in code to an iPhone. Apple politely declined and the FBI had to find a way to prosecute the case without Apple's help. Modern encryption techniques are so secure that the Federal Bureau of Investigation can't even get past them.

My buddy Jarod is an amazing mechanic. He can tell what's wrong with your car just by listening to it. He and his wife decided to start a business working on cars. She would keep the books and deal with the customers and he used his talents to get people on the road again. He started out working on cars right out of his own garage. Word spread quickly because when he fixed a car it stayed fixed. And their prices were fair. Soon they were able to buy a building and even hire employees.

One day they got a letter stating their business was under investigation for tax fraud. I was astounded. This was the most honest guy I'd ever met. He and his wife were shocked to find out their personal bank accounts and credit cards were frozen along with any accounts associated with the business.

After eight long grueling months, it turned out the IRS had made the error. But the damage had already been done. Not only did the family have psychological trauma from the incident, there were financial consequences as well. They had gotten behind on bills and lost their good reputation for always paying on time. The business suffered too. Because payments were delayed, orders for parts were cancelled. Clients were lost. It was a mess. They wanted to sue the IRS but that would cost more money and the IRS has unlimited resources to fight a court battle like that. He and his family just tried to pick up the pieces and move forward as best they could. It was very hard.

Imagine calling an attorney for help because you're being falsely accused. Now you have to tell the lawyer you have no way to pay because all of your assets have been frozen. Something tells me that's going to be a short meeting.

Do you think your bank account is secure? One signature from a sleazy judge and your money is gone. Credit cards cancelled. They can even take belongings from your house. If an incompetent government agency makes a mistake, you are left with nothing.

Or wait, are you? What about those bitcoins you bought a few years ago? The government can't touch those, because you are the only one who has the encryption keys. No corrupt judge, no inept government agency, nobody can access your bitcoin except YOU!

I know that Bitcoin has a reputation for being some kind of 'criminal currency'. Believe me, I am not trying to perpetuate that stereotype. Bitcoin is a tool that we can use to protect ourselves from unruly judges and unskilled government employees.

WHAT IS BITCOIN

It used to be that the only thing we could truly own were our inner thoughts. Well, through the power of modern cryptography, we can add something else to that list. Now we can own our thoughts, and our bitcoin!

So, why is Bitcoin so secure? It's simple. Because its security system isn't located in one place, or on one server. It's distributed across millions of computers all over the world.

Before discussing this distribution network, let's talk about Microsoft Windows. We all know that Windows is one type of operating system that can run a personal computer. It's the software that tells the hardware what to do.

Now, let's say Microsoft sees a problem with Windows, something that needs to be updated. Once the programmers create the update it is sent out across the world so that every copy of Windows can be updated. If you have a Windows PC you've probably seen a message or two saying that Windows needs to be updated. The main copy of windows is kept on a central server and it has the ability to send out updates across the world. That's great, unless something goes seriously wrong with the main copy. Then you have a real problem.

Well, now imagine a different system where there is no central server. No main copy of Windows. Once you start installing Windows on computers all over the world, that's it. Each copy of Windows can talk to other active copies of Windows but there is no primary source. Everything is distributed. The downside to this system is it's almost impossible to make a universal update. The upside is, if anyone wanted to hack Windows, they would have to change every PC in the world. A big task.

Bitcoin is set up so that there is no central server. There is no 'main copy' of the Bitcoin program. You may have heard of Bitcoin miners. There are millions of 'mining computers' all across the globe. Each miner has an exact copy of the original Bitcoin software. Anyone can examine the source code. It's designed to never be updated or changed, or hacked.

Between distributed source code and advanced encryption, you can begin to see why Bitcoin is considered un-hackable.

THE GAMERS ALREADY GET IT

The year was 1999. I was working for a large satellite TV provider. Rumors were starting about a new computer game called Ever Quest. It could be played over the internet. I could sit in my basement and interact with people around the world in a virtual world using customizable characters. Each character was controlled by another player, also probably sitting in their basement. We could explore the countryside, create alliances, fight computer controlled characters, and even fight each other. The more I played, the more skilled I became. If I pillaged a village and took all the gold I could use that gold to buy better armor, weapons and maybe even a horse to ride.

I was fascinated. I installed the game on my computer and set up my account. A whole world was opened up to me. The graphics were incredible. Before I knew it, the character I had created was exploring this breathtaking virtual world with forests and trails that led to lakes and streams and even the virtual oceans. When I pressed the up arrow, my character moved forward, the back arrow he moved backwards. When I moved the mouse around, he looked around in different directions. I had complete control. There was a castle with a large courtyard and marketplace with armed guards. As long as I was near the castle I was safe. If anyone tried to rob me or kill me the guards protected me. As I ventured away from the castle, into the forest, I became more vulnerable. At first I could only kill small bats and rodents, but with each kill I gained strength and experience in the game. Soon I was able to kill stray wolves, then bears, then giant mutant spiders and so on. As I explored and killed and pillaged I got more and more money. Game money. Gold, silver and bronze coins that I could trade for, well, anything. But then it happened. A robber came along and killed me. And took all my money! I could bring my character back to life, but all that money I had worked so hard for was gone! I about lost interest in the game. But then a friend at work told me about a bank, in the game. What? How did I miss this? Sure enough I went back to the market near the castle and there it was. A bank. I could keep my coins there and then go back to hunting. If I got robbed they could only take what I was carrying at the time. I could go to my bank and everything I had saved was still there. This changed everything.

Now I could kill and pillage, kill and pillage and save my winnings. I was getting richer and richer by the minute.

As I got more money, weapons and skills I was able to go on better adventures and kill bigger monsters. The game became even more fun.

Then I heard about someone at work earning money playing Ever Quest. Not game money. The real thing. I was intrigued. Apparently they were selling their characters to people who didn't have the time to build a character up from scratch and wanted to start out with lots of money, weapons and skills. That way they could go on the better adventures right from the start. I heard someone actually sold a character for a thousand bucks! That's right, U.S. Dollars!!!

Now, let's think about this for a second. Someone traded virtual money that doesn't exist in the real world for fiat money that they can use out here in reality. Wow! What a concept. An early form of virtual money was born.

As I said, this is a non-technical description of Bitcoin. I haven't gone back on that statement, but there are a few specifications you need to know before you can truly understand the overall concept of Bitcoin. First, there are twenty-one million bitcoins in existence. There will never be any more or any less than twenty-one million. This is how it was designed and it cannot be changed. Each bitcoin can be split into much smaller units, but we don't need to worry about that for the purposes of this book. Just keep in mind the amount of bitcoins cannot be changed.

At its root, Bitcoin is basically a ledger. A very large ledger. Kind of like the ledger you see on your bank statement each month. Except this ledger keeps track of every Bitcoin transaction that has ever and will ever take place. It's amazing to think that one single ledger that large could be maintained, and in fact that is one of the most incredible aspects of Bitcoin. Every time someone buys or sells Bitcoin, that transaction must be verified by mining computers all around the world. Once the transaction is verified, it is made a permanent part of the ledger. Forever.

I won't lie. Each time I buy or sell a bitcoin I think about everything going on behind the scenes. I remember watching old black and white movies when I was young. Sometimes there would be a scene where someone is going to meet with a banker. The banker would be dressed up in a suit and tie sitting behind a desk. If a transaction needed to be recorded, the banker would pull out a large book and pull it open with both hands. He would dab a quill pen in ink and then make a notation.

If it helps to envision something in the real world that can be easily related to Bitcoin, just think about a banker keeping a bank log. The miners are the bankers and the bank log is distributed among all the miners.

Another analogy that helps is to imagine a video game with a bank vault containing safety deposit boxes. Let's say there are twenty-one million boxes in the fault, each box contains a bitcoin.

If a customer buys a safety deposit box from this virtual bank they are given the key to that specific box. Even the bank owner can't get into it without the key. The banker only gives out one key. The box is in the vault and the key is in the customer's hand.

Now give that a minute to sink in. Think about the responsibility. If you lose that key, you lose the bitcoin. The bank doesn't have any duplicates and the lock Is unbreakable. One key, one lock. If the Army, Navy, Marines, Air Force, the Supreme Court, the U S President, the Senate, the House (you get the idea) all united together wanted to get inside that vault, inside that box, they couldn't. Not unless you give them the key. That's a lot of power. Remember the movie Ghostbusters? The Bitcoin network is the 'gatekeeper' and you are the 'key master'. The government can track bitcoin. Yes, they know you have it, but nobody, and I mean nobody has access to that bank box except you unless they get your key. Now you may have heard about law enforcement agencies confiscating bitcoins. They have to get the codes first, no way around it. If you hand that key to someone, you lose all the power. You transfer ownership to that person. Am I encouraging illegal activity? Absolutely NOT! I am saying that we can use Bitcoin to protect ourselves from a corrupt government.

What if you make a copy of the key? That's actually a good question. I'm glad you asked it. In that case, whoever makes it to the vault first can claim the bitcoin inside the box. The first one there can sell the bitcoin and convert it into fiat money. They could then buy another bitcoin and they will get a new key. At that point the old key and any copies would be useless.

Now, of course the vault and lock and box are all virtual. The key is a code that can be kept in a text file. That is yours. Everything else out on the Internet. But is it real? Oh yes. It's real.

The main thing to take away from this chapter is that once you are assigned a bitcoin key, it's very important to keep it safe. The bitcoin ledger keeps track of which keys unlock which bitcoin. It does not keep track of what people have what keys. Whoever has the key, has all the power.

THE COMMUNITY

I've been a Star Trek fan since I was a kid. I love the vision of Star Trek. In the Star Trek universe everyone on earth has everything needed to build a good life. That's the world I would love to live in. Fundamental needs are all met, and access to the tools and resources necessary to build a good life are easily available.

Right now, the world we live in has so much disparity. Some people have more than anyone could imagine and opportunities are boundless. Others don't even have a reliable money system. People in those areas try to barter, but as we discussed earlier, that doesn't work very well.

Imagine if you want to be a business owner and you live in a country with no reliable form of money. How will you pay your employees? Eggs? That's not going to work very well.

Imagine walking into a store with a wallet full of money. When you are ready to pay the cashier politely says 'Sorry, we don't accept money anymore.' That wallet, that money is useless. We can't imagine something like that here in the United States, but in other countries that's a reality.

Bitcoin changes all that. Anyone with access to the Internet can not only buy bitcoin, but also accept bitcoin as payment. If you live in a country where the money system collapsed, don't worry, because Bitcoin isn't based on any one country. It's a global currency.

We should all do what we can to make life better for everyone on Earth and most people are very charitable. Sometimes it's difficult though. How do you know if you can trust the charity program? The best thing we can do is support systems and programs that are going to benefit everyone.

The people who have worked to get Bitcoin where it is today are true visionaries. They saw what it could do for the global economy very early on and worked very hard to make it a reality. Now that it's being more widely adopted, the true benefits of Bitcoin are going to be seen more and more.

If Bitcoin is allowed to grow to its full potential, and I believe it will, it could greatly reduce poverty and suffering around the world. Once people have a reliable money system that cannot be corrupted by governments, large banks, or politicians they can build on that basic foundation. Then life will get better and better, everywhere.

Bitcoin is more than just a lucrative investment. Its hope for a brighter future, for all of us. Remember one of the main reasons salt is no longer used as money. It has become too abundant. We've figured out too many ways to get salt. Technical advancement made salt almost worthless. Well, that will never happen with Bitcoin. Since there are a set number of bitcoins that will never change we don't have to worry about it ever becoming overly abundant.

WHAT IS REAL?

If someone came up to you and said 'The Internet isn't real. It's fake', how would you respond? You'd probably think they had a few too many morning cocktails. I mean let's face it. The internet is very real. We rely on it for...well...just about everything. But if they pushed the issue, how would you convince them they are wrong?

Visionaries like you and I are being faced with the same questions regarding Bitcoin. Someone might walk up to you while you right now and ask, 'What are you reading?' When you tell them they might say something like 'Oh, Bitcoin. That's nonsense. It's not real.' Hopefully you've gained enough from this book to make a logical argument to the contrary. But it's not easy. I have a few theories on what people perceive to be real and fake. To me, the more useful something is, the more real it becomes. Back in the late eighties, if you told someone the Internet is fake, they would probably just take your word for it. But the Internet has become so incredibly useful and has intertwined itself into so many aspects of our lives that now the statement just doesn't make sense.

As Bitcoin becomes more useful, it will become more real.

GOVERNMENTS AND BANKS

This chapter is going to get a little dicey. If you end up disagreeing with anything I say, that's okay. All I ask is that you hear me out. Here we go. I'm going to start by making two bold statements.

First, 'Large banks are evil.' Okay, that wasn't so hard.

Second, 'Elected officials are easily corrupted.' Whew! I did it. Now that we've got that out of the way, let me explain why those statements are important to Bitcoin.

To be fair, I'm only talking about large banks. You know the ones 'too big to fail'?

The smaller, local banks and credit unions try to help their local communities. I'm not talking about them.

Large banks receive freshly printed money from the treasury at a low or zero percent interest rate. Free money. These banks are then supposed to circulate that money out to the general public through low interest loans. On paper it seems like a pretty good system. Everybody benefits. But the evil banks are greedy. They decide they don't want to circulate the money. They want to keep it for themselves.

Regular people like you and I can't pay 200% interest every year. If the banks circulate the money out to us like they are supposed to, they won't make very much in return. The banks want to keep the money and use it to buy things. Lucrative things. Casinos, shopping malls, condominiums, theme parks. They want to double or triple their assets every year! That's when they form a very wicked plan. They meet with creepy, icky politicians and make an evil agreement.

If the elected officials will simply vote to lower banking regulations the banks will use their incredible riches to fund the politician's next campaign election.

Next thing you know the banks are only required to lend a tiny fraction of the money they receive from the treasury and they get to play with the rest. Then, because of huge campaign contributions, the same lousy politicians get elected over and over again. What a perfectly villainous plan. Bitcoin is going to bring an end to it.

Now that you are reading this book, you should pay closer attention to the news. I have a website that keeps track of all the latest Bitcoin developments. Please feel free to visit www.cybermoolah.com anytime. You might notice that banks and elected officials are very afraid of Bitcoin. There's a good reason for that. The very people who promised to keep our money safe ended up taking all the money for themselves. Bitcoin is going to ruin all their sinister plans. Once Bitcoin becomes the primary world currency, we won't need the government to print money for us. We also won't need the banks to circulate anything. They will just have to find some other way to steal our money. It might turn them into honest people. But, let's not get our hopes up.

Do you have some money in your wallet right now? If you do, please take it out and look at it. Now, ask yourself, 'Does that money belong to me?'

It doesn't. I know. It's strange. Even though it's in your wallet. You earned it, right? But it's not yours. The government and large banks actually have more control over that money than you do. They influence its value. They can take it away from you anytime they want. That money belongs to the government and the large banks and believe me they don't want you or me to have any of it and they work very hard to make sure it stays out of our hands.

If there is one thing I want you to keep in mind after reading this book, besides having a good understanding of Bitcoin, it is this. That money in your wallet is government money. It belongs to them. Bitcoin is the people's money. It belongs to regular, ordinary people. It belongs to you and me. Bitcoin is truly ours and the government can't influence it or take it away from us.

Bitcoin is the money of the people. Please remember that.

Fiat money is so corrupt and harmful they might as well put demonic markings all over the dollar bill. Oh, wait. They already did.

If that money in your wallet truly belonged to the people, would it look so ugly and devilish? No. If it truly belonged to the people it would have a beautiful scene printed on it. Maybe a Bob Ross paining or something. Now, THAT would be some cool money!

PLANES, TRAINS, MICROCHIPS AND AUTOMOBILES

I wasn't sure where to put this chapter in the book. I suppose it could go anywhere, but to me it's one of the most important chapters. Some people might be alarmed when they read the title to chapter nine. It's very important to read this chapter first. I want to make sure you understand just how amazing cryptocurrency is before we start talking about aliens.

If I asked you to write down the world's top five discoveries or inventions, think for a minute about what you might include. I'm sure automobile and airplane would be on the list. Maybe electricity, the computer, or microchip. You might pick trains, or the steam engine. There are many choices. But would you include Bitcoin? My guess is you probably would not immediately think of that as being one of the world's greatest inventions, but I would argue Bitcoin is the greatest discovery of all.

Hold on. Don't turn on me. We haven't even gotten to the alien connection. Let me make my case. How do we decide if an invention or discovery is 'great'? Isn't it the impact it has on the world? The greatest discoveries have the largest impact. That makes sense. To be fair, Bitcoin is still in its infant stages. It has not had the chance to make its full mark on the world. When it does, it will completely eclipse any other invention or discovery. Just like people had a hard time finding a use for the personal computer, Bitcoin will have to go through its own awkward adolescence. There will be complications and setbacks, but it will eventually establish itself as the safest, most reliable form of currency on the planet.

THE ALIEN CONNECTION

Here it is. You made it. You've been looking forward to this chapter for a while now. As you read the previous chapters it was in the back of your head, wasn't it? 'Alien connection? What?'

Yep. I think Bitcoin is a gift from a more advanced, alien civilization and I will tell you why.

What's your favorite software application? Is it a word processor, a spreadsheet? Maybe you're a graphics designer so you LOVE image editors. Whatever it is, no matter how popular and functional your favorite software may be, I guarantee it had to evolve to the point where it is now. Every popular, functional piece of software ever written has had to be corrected and changed over time. Version 1.0, then 1.1, eventually 2.0 and so on. Even Albert Einstein's famous theory of relativity was originally released with an error. He later changed the equation to e = mc squared. But it was too late. He had already published the original, flawed version. So, what we have now is the theory of relativity 2.0. Nothing comes out of the box perfect. Well...except Bitcoin that is.

I'm not trying to make fun of Albert Einstein by the way. I'm just making a point. Everything created by Earthlings has to go through an evolutionary stage. Even the other crypto coins that came after Bitcoin are already having to be revised. At the time of this publication there is talk of releasing Ethereum 2.0. Same with Cardano. Why hasn't there been a Bitcoin 2.0? There never will be. Bitcoin was developed and perfected on another planet, maybe even another galaxy. It evolved somewhere else. Maybe it's been passed from planet to planet over millions of years. The philanthropic alien scientists who originally developed it on their own home world have watched it transform other civilizations for the better and whenever a planet reaches a certain state of technological advancement (assuming they haven't blown themselves up yet) they offer Bitcoin as a gift, from their world to ours.

Here's a question I want you to think long and hard about. Why would the creator of Bitcoin stay anonymous? That's right, nobody actually knows who invented, or wrote the original design for Bitcoin. What reason would this person have to hide their identity? The creators of other cyber coins, which have been basically copied from Bitcoin, are considered celebrities. Everybody loves them. There would be no reason for the original creator of Bitcoin to hide, unless this person doesn't want us to know it's actually a technology from another world. The same world that Dolly Parton is from. Dolly couldn't possibly be from Earth. She's too amazing. But that's a subject for another book.

Also, Bitcoin is too good. It's too helpful. People on this planet are selfish. Even discoveries that have been beneficial to society, still made the creator rich. There is no patent on Bitcoin. The source code can be downloaded and examined, even copied and changed to make other coins by anyone savvy enough to understand it. That's not how we do things here on this planet. We're constantly trying to claw our way to the top of the heap, where the air is cleaner so we can look down on anybody who didn't make it to the top like we did. I'm sorry but it's true.

You might be thinking 'Wait Anthony. What about penicillin?' Okay, yes it's true, the man who developed penicillin released the patent to the public. But he didn't do it anonymously. He was still regarded as a public hero for the rest of his life.

Now, Earthlings definitely had a hand in implementing Bitcoin. There are many people who worked very hard to get Bitcoin up and running. But they didn't design it. They didn't create it. To this day Bitcoin remains a gift from an anonymous genius, I believe from another world.

CYBER MOOLAH

Okay so now when 'that friend' walks up and asks you what Bitcoin is you can give them this book and tell them to read it or you can give them the short, simple answer. Here it is...

Bitcoin is property.

Yep. At the end of the day that's all it really is. It's an amazing new form of property that's going to make the world a better place. But, it's still just property and just like any other property the value of it can go up or down or remain unchanged. Now, if that friend persists and says 'But property is real. Bitcoin isn't real.' Just tell them it's as real as the Internet.

If they bug you any further, unfriend them.

So, as I stated at the beginning, I wrote this book in an effort to make more people aware of Bitcoin and give a fundamental, and non-technical understanding of it. Only you can be the judge of my success.

As an additional resource, I've started a website to help anyone who is interested keep up to date on the most recent changes in the crypto world. Please visit cybermoolah.com to find videos and articles ranging from technical analysis to recent developments. It's updated daily with the most recent information. Even if you decide Bitcoin isn't for you and you never buy a single satoshi, at least you can say you understand the concept and you are making an informed decision.

BOOKS BY THIS AUTHOR

Zombie Planet

The Scarfts were an ordinary family in every way until Mr. Scarft made a discovery in his physics lab. Now they can easily travel anywhere in the universe. Deep space is stranger and more dangerous than any of them ever thought. With great power comes great responsibility. They are seeing things that defy even their wildest imaginations. The first habitable planet they land on seems to be a paradise. Everything's great until they find out the local inhabitants are being regularly attacked by zombies! Join the Scarft family on this fascinating adventure.

The Amulet Stone

The Scarft family seem perfectly normal, even a little boring to their neighbors in rural Pocatello, Idaho. They've been trying very hard to keep their new discovery a secret. They now have the ability to travel anywhere in the universe, instantly and effortlessly. They have already embarked on several exciting adventures and met Scotty and his crew, explorers from planet Atlantis. They were astonished to find out that the ancient ancestors of Atlantis once lived on Earth! As a token of friendship Scotty gave the Scarfts a super advanced computer system named Beverly. With Beverly's help the Scarfts are learning new, incredible things every day. Beverly needs assistance with a project that is very important to her and she must betray the confidence of the leaders of Atlantis, her home planet. She convinces the oldest child, Tony, to join her on a secret mission that could ruin the new friendship forming between the Scarfts and people of Atlantis, and possibly even jeopardize stability within the universe as a whole. While on this dangerous mission Tony and Beverly make a discovery that changes everything. What they uncover challenges even the most basic understandings of life and the universe. They learn the answer to the age old question, where did we come from? Join them on this astonishing and fast paced adventure.

Playing Slot Machines

Increase your chances of winning at slot machines. This book takes you step by step through everything from picking the right casino, to finding the machine that's most likely to pay out. Also, learn the tricks to game play that will help you defeat the most modern casinos.

Made in the USA
Columbia, SC
08 April 2025